I Try New Things.
I Am
CONFIDENT!

My Amazing Toddler
Behavioral Series

An Affirmation-Themed
Pre-K Confidence Book (Ages 2-4)

By

Suzanne T. Christian

TWORAVENS
B O O K S

Two Little Ravens
CHILDREN'S NON-FICTION BOOKS

Paperback Edition: 9781964202204
Hardcover Edition: 9781964202211
Digital Edition: 9781964202228

Published in the United States by Two Ravens Books LLC,
254 Chapman Rd, Ste 209, Newark DE 19702

'Expand the mind, free the imagination, one title at a time.'
www.tworavensbooks.com

Welcome to
"I Try New Things. I Am Confident!"

This book is a delightful collection of easy-to-understand affirmations designed specifically for young children. As you explore its pages together, your child will learn the importance of confidence, bravery, and a positive mindset.

Each page features vibrant illustrations and relatable scenarios, encouraging your child to enjoy new experiences. By making this book a regular part of your reading routine, you can witness a gradual boost in your toddler's confidence, as repetition is a proven teaching tool.

Prepare for a journey of self-discovery, courage, and lots of fun with your little one!

Suzanne T. Christian

Trying new things is fun!

I can put on
my shoes all
by myself.

When I fall down,
I get back up and smile.

Making new friends
makes me happy.

Painting with
my fingers is
so much fun.

Tasting new foods is yummy.

I build tall towers with my blocks.

When I try,
I can do
anything.

I try and try
until I can do it.

I picked out my clothes.
Today, I wear spots and stripes!

I can put on my jacket.
I am confident!

I brush my teeth,
swish, swash!

I stand on stage and sing my song. Everyone claps along!

I explore the
backyard jungle.
Roar! I'm a
brave lion.

I try the big kid swing. Up, up, and away!

I say "hello" to
new friends at
the park.
We play and
laugh together.

I help bake cookies. Mixing dough is messy and fun.

I tell a silly joke.
Everyone giggles.
I am confident!

New places are
fun to see.

I ride
my bike fast.
Zoom!
Look at me go!

I am strong.
I am brave.
I am confident!

I try new things.
I am confident!

The End!

My Amazing Toddler Behavioral Series

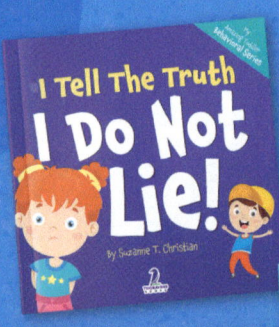

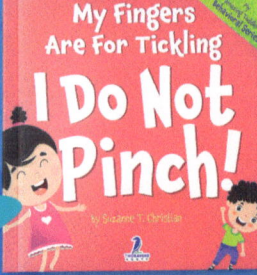

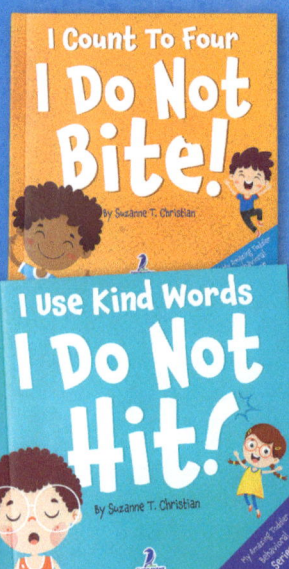

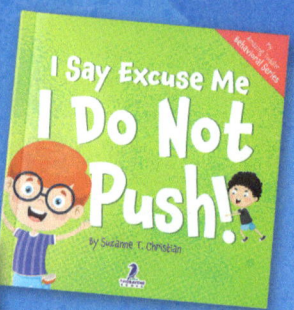

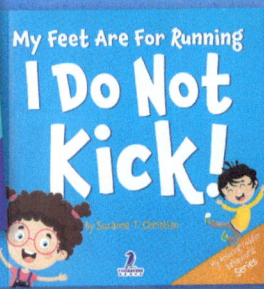

Check Out
Suzanne T. Christian's beloved series
'My Amazing Toddler Behavioral Series'.
Young readers are sure to enjoy!

Two Little Ravens

CHILDREN'S NON-FICTION BOOKS

Dear Amazing Reader,

Thank you for diving into **I Try New Things. I Am Confident!** with me. If this book touched your heart or made a difference for a young reader, I'd be grateful if you could share your thoughts in a review. Your feedback inspires my future work and helps others discover the magic within these pages.

I'd love to hear from you directly if you have suggestions or ideas for improving the book. Please feel free to reach out to me at **suzanne.christian@tworavensbooks.com.** Your voice counts, and I cherish it deeply.

With heartfelt gratitude,

www.ingramcontent.com/pod-product-compliance
Lightning Source LLC
Chambersburg PA
CBHW041600120626
46551CB00002B/269